HOW TO IMPROVE AT MAKING
JEWELLERY

Sue McMillan

CONTENTS

2

INTRODUCTION

Since prehistoric times, humans have worn jewellery to decorate their bodies, ward off evil spirits, or to show people that they belong to a group or hold an important position. Bead jewellery has been worn by people for tens of thousands of years – the earliest examples of this kind of jewellery were made from snail shells.

GETTING CREATIVE

The wonderful thing about jewellery making is that, once you have learned the basic techniques, there is no limit to the pieces you can design. There are so many styles and materials that you can really let your imagination go wild!

You need some basic tools and materials. But if you are on a limited budget, you can keep costs down by hunting for old jewellery in second-hand shops. You will find that you can re-use many of the pieces, such as beads and fasteners.

GUIDE TO STEPS

In this book, we will show you step-by-step how to make many different pieces, including necklaces, bracelets and earrings, using a variety of materials.

The process is broken down into manageable steps, showing you the most important techniques for making pieces, from attaching clasps to making your own beads.

Once you have mastered these examples, you can use your new skills to design fabulous pieces of unique jewellery!

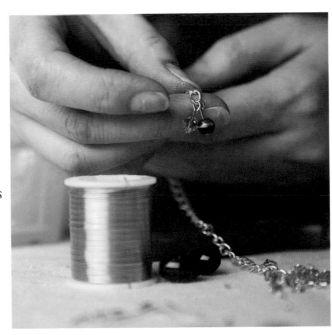

A HISTORY OF JEWELLERY

Jewellery has a long and varied history. The oldest form were necklaces, probably made 75,000 years ago with snail shell beads. Other prehistoric necklaces and bracelets were made with bone, teeth and stones. Later, jewellery makers created imaginative pieces with gem stones or precious metals. Today, jewellery uses all the materials of the past, as well as many that have only become available recently.

PREHISTORY

In Africa, jewellery has been discovered that dates from the Stone Age. These simple snail shells were found in South Africa. The shells have holes in them and traces of ochre pigment, which suggests that they were once strung together as necklaces. The ochre was either used to decorate the shell, or rubbed off from the skin of the wearer.

4

ANCIENT EGYPT

By the time of the Ancient Egyptians, 3,000 years ago, jewellery making was an established craft. The Egyptians used a lot of gold, semi-precious stones such as lapis lazuli and turquoise, and coloured glass. Different colours and stones had different meanings. As well as being used to convey wealth and status, many pieces of Egyptian jewellery had symbols that were thought to protect the wearer.

ANCIENT GREECE

In Ancient Greece, jewellery was also made from gold, semi-precious stones and glass. The type of jewellery that the Greeks are most well known for creating is the portrait cameo (right). Greek jewellery was mostly simple and was worn for special occasions rather than used every day.

THE ROMAN EMPIRE

The Romans were very fond of jewellery. The most common article was the brooch, or fibula, which was used to pin clothing. Roman jewellery was made from a variety of metals, and was highly decorated with precious and semi-precious stones. Wealthy Roman women wore necklaces (left), bracelets, earrings, rings and hairpins. Men usually wore only one ring.

CELTIC DESIGN

In the centuries after the Roman Empire, many cultures continued to create stunning pieces of jewellery. The Celts created abstract designs and wore torques, twisted metal collars or armbands (right), used to protect the wearer. In medieval times, only the wealthiest were permitted to wear gold and silver. Many pieces showed religious scenes, painted on with enamels.

DESIGN AND CHANGE

From the 17th century, the advance in cutting techniques meant that gems, especially diamonds, could be used in many pieces in a wide variety of different styles. By the 19th century, floral motifs were popular, until the Art Deco movement took over in the 1930s. Jewellers began to create geometric pieces featuring a mixture of many gemstones.

INTO THE FUTURE

Modern-day jewellery uses many different materials, from traditional metals and gemstones, to beads, plastic and glass. Jewellery is seen by many as wearable art, and they use it to identify with a particular group. Many people have started to make their own jewellery.

JEWELLERY AROUND THE WORLD

Most pieces of jewellery are of value only to the wearer and do not cost a lot. But some pieces have become famous because they are so expensive or very beautiful. Some of these have an amazing story behind them. Others are well known because they are perfect examples of jewellery making as an art.

TUTANKHAMUN

More than 150 intricate pieces of jewellery were discovered in the tomb of the pharaoh Tutankhamun. Many are the finest examples of Ancient Egyptian jewellery found to date. This vulture pectoral, or collar, was around the mummy's neck.

LALIQUE

René Lalique (1860–1945) produced some of the finest pieces of Art Nouveau jewellery, which are prized by collectors for their beautiful design and craftsmanship. The moonstones and opals in this dragonfly give it a shimmering, mystical quality.

FABERGÉ

When Carl Fabergé (1846–1920) is mentioned, most people think of the jewelled eggs that he created for the Russian tsars. However, he also created many stunning pieces of jewellery, including a famous diamond tiara which sold for over £1 million at auction recently.

Globally, there is a huge range of styles of jewellery, as well as a great variety of materials used. The reasons for adorning the body tend to be universal. However, different countries and societies create their own 'look'.

AFRICA

In Africa, jewellery has been made from all sorts of materials, including metal, seeds and bone. Possibly the most striking pieces are the intricate beaded patterns worn by the Masai tribe (left) during special occasions such as weddings.

KAYAN NECK RINGS

In Myanmar, women of the Kayan tribe traditionally wear brass neck rings. Gradually adding these rings pushes down the collarbone to extend the length of the neck. No one is sure how this unusual and unique custom started.

INDIA & INDONESIA

India has a long tradition of jewellery making, particularly with gold. Traditionally, Hindu women have to wear sixteen things, including necklaces, bindi (a forehead decoration) and bangles. In Indonesia, silver is a very popular metal for jewellery.

NATIVE AMERICANS

Native Americans have a long tradition of using horn, bone, beads, feathers and leather to produce striking pieces of jewellery of many kinds.

SYMBOLISM

Throughout history jewellery has had symbolic meaning. Probably the most well known is the wedding ring, traditionally worn on the third finger of the left hand. It was thought that the veins in this finger led directly to the heart.

MEMBERSHIP

Some pieces of jewellery identify the wearer as belonging to a group. Probably the most common of these are the ones that represent religion. Some Christians, for example, wear a crucifix to show their faith, while Jewish people sometimes wear the Star of David. Many people also carry rosary beads.

COMMITMENT

In some cultures, before marriage, an engagement ring is given to the woman to show that a couple are betrothed. In Ireland, Claddagh rings were given as a token of love.

FRIENDSHIP

Some bracelets are made using embroidery thread. They are often exchanged as a sign of friendship. Traditionally, the bracelet should be worn until it wears out or falls off.

CHARM BRACELETS

These are simple chain bracelets, to which charms can be added. Usually a wearer will choose charms that have a personal meaning. Often they are added to symbolize important events in a person's life, such as the birth of a baby.

STATUS

Some items of jewellery are worn to show status. Throughout history, kings and queens have worn gold and jewels to show their position as the richest and most powerful people in their country. Queen Elizabeth I of England is shown here wearing lots of jewels. Gold chains of office are worn by some officials, including mayors, as symbols of power and authority.

PROTECTION

In many cultures, jewellery is worn to protect the wearer from evil. In parts of the Middle East and Mediterranean, charms with an eye symbol were used to ward off the bad luck from the 'evil eye' – a bad look or a stare. In some places, the evil eye charm is still used today.

BEADS

Bead threading is one of the oldest and most straightforward forms of jewellery making. Today, beads come in a dazzling array of materials including glass, plastic, clay and metal, and are available in every colour of the rainbow.

TYPES OF BEAD

BOHEMIAN GLASS – Almost limitless in range, these include round, faceted and fire-polished designs and come in many different shapes, including hearts, stars and flowers.

BUGLE – These long, tube-shaped beads are available in lengths from 2mm to 30mm. The most common lengths are 3mm, 6mm and 9mm.

CERAMIC – Use these beads to add contrast, as they usually have a matt texture.

CUBE – These square-shaped beads can be used to add extra interest to designs. The most common size is 4mm.

MAGATAMA DROPS – These beads have a large hole and are very useful for adding texture and depth to designs.

METAL – These small spacer beads, usually silver or gold, are great for adding some sparkle to your design.

SEED – These small, glass beads have a central hole, usually 2mm in diameter. They are sometimes called 'rocailles'.

SHELL PENDANTS

Pendants made from natural materials, such as these shells, make eye-catching focal points for your pieces of jewellery. Their variation in colour and pattern will allow you to make truly unique pieces.

TOP TIP

Check the ends of bugle beads, discarding any that are sharp or cracked, as they may cut the thread.

STORAGE

There are many ways to store your beads. The most convenient is in storage boxes (below right) that have separate compartments, so that the beads can be sorted by type and colour. When working, triangular dishes (below left) will help you to organize what you need.

EQUIPMENT AND OTHER TOOLS

To make bead jewellery, there are a number of basic tools that you need. Some you will already have around the home, while others can be sourced from craft shops or online from specialist suppliers.

WIRE – There are many different types of wire available. You can choose by colour, gauge (thickness) and strength. For designs that need to hold their shape, choose a lower gauge. If you need a flexible, delicate look, choose a higher gauge.

ACRYLIC PAINTS – For projects in which you want to paint jewellery, acrylic paints, a natural sponge, sponge brush or bristle brush are essential.

RIBBONS, WIRES AND THREAD – A number of different materials can be used. Collect ribbons, cords, braids, elastic and fishing line, so that you can experiment with different finishes. Shells are also useful, if you can source them.

A MEASURING TAPE AND RULER – Useful for checking thread, cord and ribbon lengths.

GLUE – Adhesives such as silicone glue are used to attach items to your jewellery. A cocktail stick can be used to accurately place tiny drops of glue.

WOODEN SPOON – An everyday item that can be used to twist wire.

SCISSORS – Essential for cutting thread, wire and ribbon.

PLIERS AND WIRE CUTTERS – Two pairs of jeweller's pliers – one long-nosed, the other round-nosed – and a pair of wire cutters are essential pieces of equipment for jewellery making.

A KEEN EYE

Keep any attractive pieces of cord, ribbon or thread you find, as they may be just the thing for a really eye-catching piece!

NEEDLES, THREAD AND FINDINGS

As well as your essential tools, there are a number of small yet vital pieces of equipment that you will need in order to start your first jewellery project. These include needles and clasps, as well as many different types of pin.

NEEDLES

Beading needles are available in many lengths, the most common being around 50mm long. The eye on beading needles is tiny, and this can make threading them a bit of a challenge. However, the smaller size allows the needle to pass through even the smallest of beads.

THREADS, CORDS AND CABLES

As well as wire, there are many different materials that you can use to thread beads. *Nymo* is a nylon beading thread, which does not twist, so your beads will hang nicely.

It is available in a number of thicknesses – B is the best for most projects. If you want to use larger beads or need firmer tension, choose D, which is thicker.

CLEAR ELASTIC CORD

This is ideal for using with any colour of bead, as it is transparent. It also has the advantage that it does not fray. It is available in three thicknesses: 0.5mm, 0.7mm and 1mm.

JEWELLERY CABLE

This soft, flexible type of wire is ideal for projects in which you need to thread beads onto a straight wire.

FINDINGS

'Findings' are the smaller pieces, such as rings and clasps, that you will need to create beaded jewellery. On this page are some of the different types you will need for the projects in this book.

1 FILIGREE BELL CAPS – These can be threaded on either side of a large glass bead to decorate it.

2 SPLIT RING – This is a double ring of wire, a bit like a very tiny key ring. It is ideal for using with a lobster clasp at the end of a bracelet or necklace.

3 JUMP RINGS – Made from a single loop of wire, these are used to attach pendants to a necklace.

4 CRIMP TUBES – Crimp tubes and crimp beads are used with jewellery cable to finish the end of the necklace. The tube or bead is squashed in place using a pair of pliers. Tubes are easier to work with than beads.

5 LOBSTER CLASPS – One of the most common and easy-to-use clasps, used with a split ring to fasten a necklace or bracelet.

6 MAGNETIC CLASPS – These pull together because of the magnets inside. They are ideal for people who find clasps difficult to fasten. NB: Magnetic clasps should not be used on jewellery if the person who will be the wearer has a pacemaker.

7 HEADPINS – These long pins with a head on one end can be used to make charms.

8 SAFETY PINS – These are very easy to use for different projects. Try threading beads onto the safety pins, then linking them to make interesting pieces. You can buy safety pins in many different sizes, the most common being 28mm and 34mm. As well as gold and silver, safety pins come in a variety of fun colours, including purple, green and blue.

STRINGING AND PREP

There are a number of basic techniques used in beading. Once you have practised and mastered them you will be able to undertake a wider variety of beading projects, creating exciting and imaginative pieces.

Before you begin any beadwork, prepare the thread by pulling it through a beeswax block, or thread conditioner, twice. This will stop the thread from fraying or tangling.

Picking up beads is trickier than it looks, so it is worth spending some time practising. Here are a couple of tips:

1

Put some of the beads on a flat surface. Place the end of the needle on the side of the bead you want to pick up. It is easier if you hold the needle at the end, as shown here. Take care to keep it as close to the work surface as possible.

2

Press down gently on the side of the bead, then flick it onto the needle, as shown. Do not worry if it takes a few goes to get this right, as it will soon become second nature!

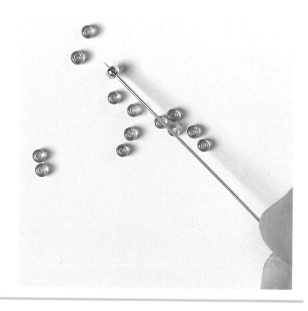

BASIC STRINGING

The easiest stringing technique is threading beads onto a length of thread. This is the oldest form of beading and the most basic technique that you have to master.

In order to create a string, it is important to use a tape measure to check how long it needs to be – in this case for a necklace. Once you are happy with the length, you can use the measurement to plan your design, spacing out the beads as shown.

STOPPER BEADS

To start a string, you first need to make a 'stopper bead' to prevent the beads from falling off the thread. First thread your needle, then take a seed bead and pass the needle through it. Now repeat this step to create a 'loop' around the bead as shown (inset left). There is no need to knot the thread. Make sure that you leave at least 10 centimetres of thread below the stopper bead.

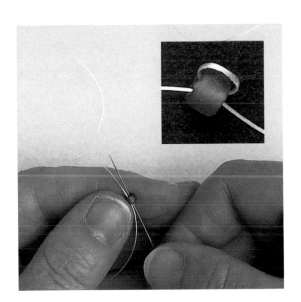

PEYOTE STITCH

Peyote stitch is a beading technique used by many cultures, including Native Americans, who often used it to decorate ceremonial items. It is a beading technique in which beads are stitched together either as flat, long strips, round shapes, or tubes. The technique can be used to make jewellery, pouches or to decorate items such as belts and ornaments. There are many types of peyote stitch – the most basic is called 'even count'.

LINKS AND WIREWORK

In addition to being used for threading, wire is also handy for creating the links, clasps and hooks that you will need for your creations. It can also be used to make whole pieces of jewellery, with just a few beads added for decoration.

FLOWER LINKS

1

For these, use 18-gauge black wire. Take a length of wire 8.5cm long and create a loop by twisting one of the ends around a pair of round-nosed pliers.

2

Make a second loop opposite the first. Now put the jaw of the pliers into the first loop, and make a third loop between the first two. Move the other jaw of the pliers into the first loop and wrap the wire again to make the fourth and final loop.

3

Use your wire cutter to trim off excess wire and finish your first flower link.

When working with wire, always wear safety goggles to protect your eyes from small pieces, which may fly off when the wire is cut.

BEADED LINK

1

These can be used to join flower links. First, cut
a 3cm length of wire and bend it at right angles
approx. 9mm from the end using long-nosed pliers.

2

Now take the round-nosed pliers and roll
the wire around the jaw to make a loop.
Thread on a bead and then make a
second loop in the same way.

HOOK CLASP

1

To make a clasp, cut a 4.4cm length of wire. Make
a simple loop at one end using round-nosed
pliers. Now use your thumb to curve the other
end of the wire around in a large loop, so that
the end comes back on the small loop.

2

Use round-nosed pliers to curl in the end
of the larger loop, so that it forms a spiral.

All of these techniques can be used in
a variety of ways. To make necklaces,
earrings or bracelets, join the bead links
and flower links together and use a hook
clasp at each end to form the closing.

ETHNIC PENDANT

The necklace is probably one of the most common items of jewellery. This attractive pendant in natural colours is a great first project, and stringing beads onto jewellery cable is quick and easy.

You will need:
- 1 shell pendant
- 150cm jewellery cable
- 96 x 4mm bronze beads
- 30 ceramic beads
- 2 silver crimp tubes
- 1 silver lobster clasp
- 1 x 7mm jump ring
- 1 x 5mm split ring
- chain-nosed pliers
- cable snips, or old scissors

1

Open the jump ring with the cable-nosed pliers. Bend the ring slightly and place it in the hole in the pendant, closing it again with the pliers.

2

Take a length of jewellery cable and use the end to pick up a silver crimp tube, followed by a lobster clasp. Bend the cable end and thread it back through the crimp tube.

3

Use the chain–nosed pliers to squash the crimp tube flat. This will secure the clasp at the end of the necklace.

4

Using the cable snips or scissors, trim the tail of the jewellery cable beyond the crimping tube so that only 1cm remains.

5

Now start threading the beads. Tuck
the remaining 1cm of the tail into the
first three bronze beads, then thread
on a ceramic bead and three more
bronze beads.

6

Continue this pattern until you have threaded
15 ceramic beads and 16 sets of bronze beads,
as shown. Now thread the pendant and
continue with the bead pattern, starting
with another set of three bronze beads.

7

Once all the
beads have
been threaded,
add the
remaining
crimp tube.
Then thread the
wire through the split ring and loop it back
through the crimp ring and two seed beads.

8

Pull the cable tight, so that the loops at the
end of the necklace are the same size, then use
chain-nosed pliers to squash the crimp tube.
Finish by trimming the excess cable close to
the bead. Now your necklace is ready to wear!

ETHNIC PENDANT

BUGLE NECKLACE

You will need:

- 135 x size 11 pink seed beads
- 86 purple 6mm bugle beads
- 42 x 4mm round, clear glass beads
- 15 x 6mm round, clear glass beads
- 2m lilac Nymo B beading thread
- 1 magnetic clasp
- beading needle
- sharp scissors

Now that you have made a single strand necklace, try a triple strand project. The bright pinks and purples work really well with the clear glass to make a really attractive piece.

1

Thread the needle with the Nymo thread, pick up five pink seed beads, the magnetic clasp, then five more pink seed beads. Push the beads and clasp down the thread to leave a 15cm tail.

2

Loop the thread, as shown, left over right, then pass the needle through the loop to make a knot. Now make a second knot, passing the thread right over left.

3

Pull the knot tight to make a ring of pink beads. Now use your

needle to pick up the beads in this order: pink seed bead, purple bugle bead, pink seed bead, 6mm glass bead, pink seed bead, purple bugle bead, pink seed bead and 4mm glass bead.

4

Repeat this pattern until you have threaded 15 x 6mm glass beads. Now pick up: pink seed bead, purple bugle, pink seed bead. Next, pick up five pink seed beads and put the needle through the free end of the clasp.

5

Pick up another five pink seed beads. Pull the thread through, then stitch back through the five pink seed beads, the clasp and the five pink seed beads from step 4.

6

Stitch back through a pink seed bead, purple bugle bead, pink seed bead, 6mm glass bead and a pink seed bead.

7

Now you add new beads by stitching through some of the first string. With your needle, pick up a purple bugle, a pink, a 4mm glass bead, a pink and a bugle. Now stitch back round the necklace, picking up a pink, a 6mm glass bead and another pink bead.

8

Repeat this along the length of the necklace until you come out of the last 6mm glass bead and stitch through a pink, a bugle and a pink.

9

Stitch through the five pink beads at the end, the clasp and the five pink beads at the other end. Go back through a pink, a bugle, 6mm glass bead and a pink.

10

Pick up: bugle, pink, 4mm glass bead, pink, bugle. Stitch through a pink, a 6mm glass and a pink. Repeat this pattern to the last 6mm glass bead, then stitch through a pink, bugle, pink. Now repeat step 9.

11

Make a loop, passing the needle under the thread, and stitch through the loop to knot. Hide the end of the thread by stitching through 3cm of beads. Snip the end, then repeat with the tail at the beginning of the necklace.

BUGLE NECKLACE

GLASS PENDANTS

Glass pendants are fascinating. They are created by firing coloured glass with metal oxides, and each piece is unique. These simple, elegant pendants are very easy to make.

You will need:
- glass pendant
- 50cm faux suede ribbon (in two colours if preferred)
- 2 flat leather crimps
- 2 jump rings
- lobster clasp
- flat-nosed pliers
- sharp scissors

1

Work out the length of the necklace, then cut the pieces of ribbon to this length.

2

Thread both lengths of ribbon through the pendant.

Murano produces some of the world's finest glasswork. It is best known for millefiori, which means 'thousands of flowers'.

3

Fix the flat leather crimps to the end of the ribbons, making sure both lengths are held in place.

4

Use pliers to attach a jump ring to each of the crimps, then attach a lobster clasp to one of the jump rings.

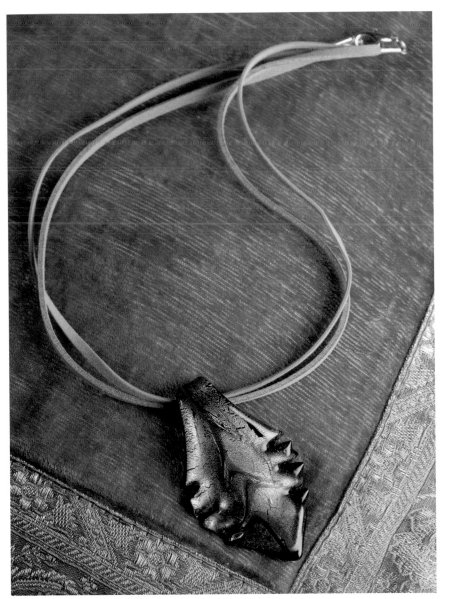

Colours

Use different colour ribbons to add an interesting contrast, or to bring out two shades in the pendant. Here, beige and turquoise have been used.

PENDANTS

Doughnut pendants can be created in a variety of designs. In this project, hand-made felt beads are used to provide a contrast with the metal.

You will need:
- 2 x pieces pink felt 2 x 3cm
- silver seed beads
- sparkly pink embroidery thread
- beading thread
- medium cotton cord
- large aluminium doughnut
- scissors
- beading needle
- sewing needle

1

Wrap the felt around a cocktail stick and use a tiny blob of fabric glue to hold it. Wind the pink embroidery thread around the felt bead. Repeat for the second bead.

2

Now slide the felt beads onto the cord, placing them almost halfway along the length.

3

Tie the cord onto the doughnut pendant, positioning the felt beads on the front.

4

Stitch some silver seed beads to the front of the felt beads.

5

Tie the cord with a slide knot, then sew clusters of seed beads to the ends for decoration.

Choose a contrasting colour for beads and felt to create a dramatic look.

Pendants, such as the Roman Amulet below, can also be added to chokers.

- memory wire choker
- size 8 seed beads
- pendant
- 2 metal feature beads
- flat-nosed pliers

1

Using pliers, bend one end of the choker wire over to make a loop.

2

Thread the seed beads on until you have almost reached the centre, then add one of the metal feature beads, the pendant and then the other metal feature bead.

27

3

Add the seed beads to the other side of the pendant, leaving 1cm at the end.

4

Bend over the wire to make another loop, and use the loops to fasten the choker in position.

Experiment with different bead and colour combinations.

OTHER NECKLACES

Yᵒᵘ can combine decorative beads, colourful pendants and cord to good effect, using a couple of simple methods.

You will need:
- doughnut pendant
- 2 decorative metal beads
- 1 metre suede ribbon
- 2 flat leather crimps
- 4 crimp beads
- 1 lobster clasp
- round-nosed pliers
- flat-nosed pliers
- scissors

1

Bring the ends of the suede ribbon together and pass them through the centre of the doughnut, leaving a loop of suede behind. Bring the ends back through the loop to knot the pendant.

2

Thread crimp beads onto each end of the suede, moving them down so that they are just above the doughnut. Secure them with the flat-nosed pliers.

3

Add a bead to each ribbon. Then add a crimp bead above each one.

Here, knots have been used instead of crimp beads.

4

Measure the necklace to the right length and trim the excess ribbon. Attach the flat leather crimps to the ends, and then fix the lobster clasp on one side.

Simple rope necklaces, decorated with shell buttons are really pretty, and they are very easy to make.

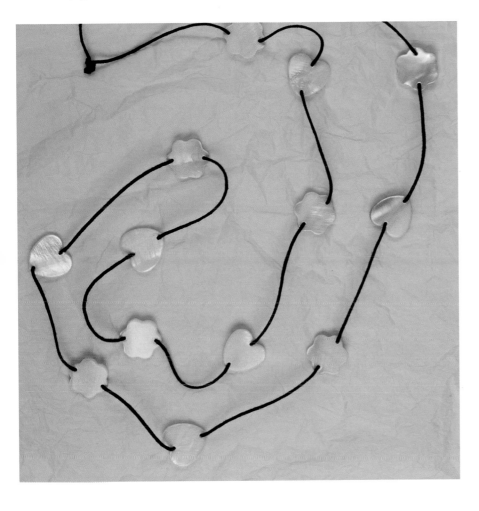

You will need:

- 1 metre stringing cord
- 14 shell buttons
- scissors

1

Measure and cut the stringing cord to the right length.

2

Thread the cord through a hole in a shell button and move it down towards the end, then thread the cord through the other hole, as shown below.

3

Continue threading the beads onto the cord, alternating the designs. Make sure you leave equal spaces between each bead.

4

Tie the cord ends in a knot to secure the rope necklace.

For a brightly coloured necklace, choose a colourful cord and contrasting beads.

OTHER NECKLACES

SAFETY PIN BRACELET

Bracelets can be simple pieces of cord, or they can be more ornate and decorated with various charms and beads. This sparkling bracelet is made from safety pins! It is easy to transform these everyday objects into a beautiful piece of jewellery.

1

Open a safety pin and thread on the following beads: pink seed bead, pink cube, pink seed bead, fire-polished bead, pink seed bead, pink cube, pink seed bead. Use only the size 8 pink seed beads on the safety pins.

2

Close the safety pin again and use the chain-nosed pliers to squash the fastening to seal it shut. Repeat steps 1 and 2 for the remaining safety pins.

3

Take the elastic cord and tie on a size 6 pink seed bead at a distance of 5cm from one end.

4

Thread on three size 6 pink seed beads, then two safety pins. Make sure you thread through the tops of the safety pins. Now add three more pink seed beads.

5

Add two more safety pins, this time threading through the bottom end. Repeat steps 4 and 5 until all the safety pins are threaded on the cord.

6

Take the second length of cord and repeat step 3, then thread it through the bottom of the end safety pin, as shown.

7

Add three pink seed beads to the thread and go through the end of the next safety pin. Thread through the end of the third safety pin, then add three more pink seed beads. Repeat this pattern all the way round, adding three seed beads after every odd numbered safety pin.

8

Remove the stopper bead, then gather the ends of the elastic together and tie them in a knot, as shown, pulling it tight. Trim the ends, then repeat the process for the second piece of elastic. Trim the ends close to the knots to complete the bracelet.

KNOTTED BRACELETS

Knotted bracelets are simple, but they are very fashionable. Use glass beads because they show up really well against the black lace.

You will need:
- 50cm black leather lacing
- 1 glass bead
- scissors

1

Wrap the lacing so that it forms a double loop, then wrap the right end over the lacing three times, threading the end back through to form a knot.

2

Thread a glass bead onto the left end and make a second knot by wrapping the end around the lacing three times, and pulling the end back through.

3

Trim the excess lacing from the knots. Use a slip knot, so the bracelet can be adjusted easily to fit.

Make several bracelets using different coloured beads. This one looks very fetching with a blue bead.

These leather bracelets have a beaded charm combined with glass and metal beads.

You will need:
- 56cm black leather lacing
- 4 green glass handmade beads
- 2 silver metal beads
- 1 metal pendant bead
- 12 x 2mm clear, silver-lined seed beads
- 8 x 4mm silver jump rings
- 1 x 8mm silver jump ring
- 2 x 6mm silver end caps
- 1 silver spring fastening
- flat-nosed pliers
- half-round-nosed pliers
- wire cutters
- scissors

1

Fold the leather lacing in half and cut it at the mid-point. Hold them together and loop them over and through to make a knot near the middle.

2

Tie a second knot 2.5cm from the other, taking care to take the lacing under and through, so that the knot faces the opposite way. Put end caps on either end of the double strand.

3

Attach 2 x 4mm jump rings and then the spring fastening to the end caps.

4

Take four head pins and thread a seed bead, glass bead and seed bead onto each. Repeat with two more pins, using metal beads. Use flat-nosed pliers to bend the head pins at right angles, and cut, leaving 1cm of wire above the beads. Bend this into a loop using the round-nosed pliers.

5

Attach the 8mm jump ring to the metal pendant bead. Divide the threaded head pins into two sets, each containing two glass beads and a metal bead. Thread each set onto a separate jump ring.

6

Link two jump rings together, then attach one set of beads to each end. Link a jump ring to one end. Attach this to the leather lacing, between the two knots. Now add the pendant bead to the final jump ring.

Choose leather lacing to tone with your beads. Brown lacing, for example, works well with pink beads.

KNOTTED BRACELETS

CHARM BRACELETS

Charm bracelets add colour to any outfit. Czech beads have a polished faceted surface, which really catches the light.

You will need:
- 16 x 50mm headpins
- jewellery cable
- 16 x size 8 clear seed beads
- 16 x size 8 turquoise seed beads
- 2 crimp tubes
- lobster clasp and 5mm split ring
- 4 x 5mm silver filigree bell caps
- 2 x 6mm dark turquoise fire-polished beads
- 2 x 6mm clear round glass beads
- 2 x 9mm turquoise matt flower beads
- 2 x 10mm turquoise disc beads
- 2 x 8mm crystal AB fire-polished beads
- 2 x 12mm turquoise AB star beads
- 2 x 10mm crystal AB heart beads
- 2 x 8mm fire-polished turquoise beads
- side cutters
- chain-nosed pliers
- 34 x 3mm silver beads
- 17 x size 5 turquoise triangle beads
- cable snips or scissors
- round-nosed pliers

34

1

Thread a clear seed bead, filigree bell cap, 6mm fire-polished bead, filigree cap and another clear seed bead. Trim the headpin, then use round-nosed pliers to make a loop, as shown.

2

Repeat this for the remaining 15 charms. You will only use the filigree bell caps for the other fire-polished bead. Note that for clear glass beads, turquoise seed beads have been used, and vice versa.

3

Cut a 30cm length of jewellery cable and thread a crimp tube and lobster clasp onto one end.

4

Thread the end of the jewellery cable back through the crimp tube, then flatten it with the pliers. Trim the end of the cable to leave a 1cm tail beyond the crimp tube.

5

Thread a 3mm silver bead, a triangle bead and another silver bead. Slide the beads down to the clasp end so they cover the trimmed end, then thread on one of the charms.

6

Repeat step 5 until all the charms are threaded. Now add a silver crimp tube and a split ring. Feed the jewellery cable end back through the crimp bead and two beads.

35

7

Squash the crimp tube with chain-nosed pliers, then trim the cable as close to the bead as possible.

FELT BEAD BRACELETS

Felt beads can be combined with wooden beads for an interesting contrast in textures.

1

Wrap the felt around a cocktail stick and use a tiny blob of fabric glue to hold it. Wind the embroidery thread around the felt bead in three sections, as shown. Now sew on seed and bugle beads. Repeat for the remaining felt beads.

2

Thread the felt beads and wooden spacer beads alternately on the elastic.

3

Keeping the elastic taut, tie a knot in the end and trim off the excess thread.

4

Gently pull the elastic so that the knot is tucked inside one of the felt beads.

For a brighter look, use pinks and purples.

Felt beads can also be used to make bangles.

You will need:

- 8 x green felt pieces 2.5 x 8cm
- iridescent green seed beads
- iridescent green bugle beads
- copper-coloured sparkly embroidery thread
- beading thread
- medium cotton cord
- scissors
- beading needle
- sewing needle

1

Wrap the felt around a cocktail stick and use a tiny blob of fabric glue to hold it. Wind the embroidery thread around the felt bead in a criss-cross pattern, as shown. Repeat for the remaining felt beads.

2

Thread the felt beads onto the cord and knot it securely to make a bangle. As this is a fixed size bangle, be sure to check the size, and if it needs to be larger, add more felt beads.

3

Gently move the knot so that it is tucked inside a felt bead. Then use a needle and embroidery thread to stitch the ends of the felt beads together.

4

Stitch bugle beads over the stitches to hide them.

5

Make a string of the seed beads, and wrap them around the bracelet. Stitch it to the cord at intervals to hold it in place.

Light and dark shades of the same colour work well for this design.

CHUNKY BEAD BRACELETS

Dramatic, bold bracelets can be created with colourful, chunky beads.

You will need:
- 9 mixed fashion beads
- 8 silver metal divider bead rings
- 2 silver drum beads
- 60cm pink faux leather lacing
- scissors
- darning needle

1

Thread the darning needle with the lacing, and add a drum bead.

2

Thread the fashion beads, alternating with the metal rings. Finish by adding the remaining drum bead.

3

Centre the beads along the lacing, so that the tails are even. To fasten, tie around the wrist in a bow.

This apple-green bracelet is ideal for spring.

Decorative toggles, or bar and ring clasps, are ideal for heavy bracelets.

You will need:
- 11 green handmade glass beads
- 11 silver eye pins
- 1 decorative ring and bar clasp
- 2 silver jump rings
- flat-nosed pliers
- half round-nosed pliers
- wire cutters

1

Thread a glass bead onto an eye pin. Use flat-nosed pliers to cut the wire 1cm above the bead.

2

Bend the wire into a loop using the round-nosed pliers. Before you close the loop, thread on another eye pin, then repeat steps 1 and 2 for the remaining beads.

3

Attach jump rings to the end eye pins. Now attach the decorative ring to one end of the bracelet and the clasp to the other.

This design is particularly attractive if metal beads are used.

CHUNKY BEAD BRACELETS

RINGS

Seed beads can be used to create a huge range of rings that are relatively easy and cheap to make. They are also perfect for using up leftover beads from other projects.

You will need:
- 1m Nymo B beading thread
- beading needle
- 60 purple size 11 seed beads
- 15 white size 11 seed beads

1

Thread the beading needle and pick up six purple seed beads, sliding them down the thread towards the end. Leave a 15cm tail.

2

Bring the needle round and stitch through the beads again in the same direction, to create a loop.

3

Pull the loop to make a little circle, then tie a reef knot – first left over right, then right over left. Pull the knot tight.

4

Pick up a white bead and stitch through the third purple bead in the circle. Then push the white bead into the centre of the circle.

5

Pick up two purple beads and one white bead and stitch through a purple bead on the right-hand side of the daisy, pulling the thread right through.

6

Pick up two purple beads and stitch through the top purple bead of your second daisy, as shown. Pull it through to complete the second flower.

7

Repeat steps 5 and 6 to make a row of daisies. Now wrap the daisies round your finger to check the length.

8

To finish your ring, pick up a purple bead on the final daisy and stitch it through two beads of the first daisy.

41

EARRINGS

Drop earrings are easy to make. By choosing matching colours and materials, you can complete jewellery sets of bracelets, necklaces and earrings.

You will need:

- 2 orange felt pieces 2.5 x 6cm
- 4 flat, black spacer beads
- 4 small gold beads
- 2 headpins
- 2 long ball wire earring hooks
- gold and yellow seed beads
- gold and yellow bugle beads
- tan embroidery thread
- beading thread
- round-nosed pliers
- flat-nosed pliers
- cutting pliers
- scissors
- beading needle
- sewing needle

1

Wrap the felt around a cocktail stick and use a tiny blob of fabric glue to hold it. Wind the embroidery thread around the felt bead in three bands, as shown. Repeat for the second felt bead. Stitch on a selection of bugle and seed beads as shown.

2

Take the headpin and thread on the following: small gold bead, flat black space, felt bead, flat black spacer, small gold bead.

3

Cut the excess wire off the headpin, leaving 1cm to bend into a loop. Attach an earring to the loop, then close it with the pliers.

4

Repeat steps 2 and 3 to make the second earring.

DRAMATIC DROP EARRINGS

Headpins can also be used as decorative pieces. Here, they have been used to make long drop earrings.

You will need:
- 2 black felt pieces 2 x 3cm
- 8 medium silver beads
- 4 small silver beads
- 4 headpins
- 2 eyepins
- 2 long ball wire earring hooks
- beading thread
- black embroidery thread
- selection of silver seed beads
- round-nosed pliers
- flat-nosed pliers
- cutting pliers
- scissors
- beading needle
- needle

1
Wrap the felt around a cocktail stick and use a tiny blob of fabric glue to hold it. Wind the embroidery thread around the felt bead in four bands, as shown. Repeat for the second bead. Stitch on a selection of bugle and seed beads as shown.

2
Take an eyepin and thread on a medium silver bead, felt bead and another medium silver bead.

3
Cut the eyepin, leaving 1cm of wire. Bend this to create a loop and attach an earring hook.

4
Thread a headpin with a seed bead, medium silver bead and a small silver bead. Cut to length and create a loop. Repeat for another headpin, this time adding three extra seed beads. Cut to length and create a loop. Attach both headpins to the bottom of the eyepin. NB: The headpins should be different lengths, as shown in the picture.

5
Repeat the process from start to finish to make the other earring.

HAIR ADORNMENTS

Striking hair decorations are simple to make using beads and wire. You can make hairbands, or twist wire around plain combs, slides or clips to give them a unique look.

You will need:
- 3m x 24 gauge silver wire
- 160 x 4mm black faceted beads
- 2 black 9 x 6mm oval beads
- black elastic
- wire cutters
- long-nosed pliers
- round-nosed pliers
- ruler
- PVA glue
- cocktail stick
- scissors

1

To make a hairband, cut two pieces of wire measuring 137cm. Hold the pieces together and twist them with your fingers, starting 5cm from one end, until you have twisted 13mm.

2

Take the 5cm tails and loop them round the round-nosed pliers. Wrap the ends around the twisted section. Trim the excess with the wire cutters.

3

Take a faceted bead. Holding the ends of the wire apart, thread the top wire down and the bottom wire up. Push the bead to the end of the wires, near the loop. Now thread two beads on the top wire, and one on the bottom.

4

Thread the bottom wire up through the second top bead, bending it round to create a cluster.

5

Measure 5mm along the wire, then thread four beads onto the bottom wire. Pull it up, round and back through the first bead to create another cluster. Repeat this with the top wire.

6

Measure 5mm down the wire, then repeat steps 3 and 4 to create another central bead cluster, then repeat step 5 to create two more clusters, as shown.

7

Repeat steps 3, 4 and 5 until the hair band is complete.

8

Tie on a piece of elastic (be sure to check the length first). Knot it, then add a dot of glue using the cocktail stick. Thread on an oval bead, pulling it down to the knot. Pull through the elastic tail then slide the bead over the glued knot. Thread on the second oval bead, then knot and glue the elastic, sliding the bead over the knot to complete the band.

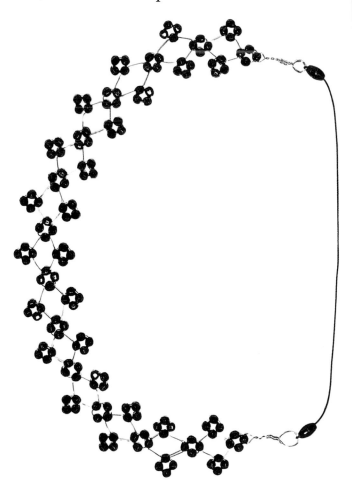

HAIR ADORNMENTS

OTHER DECORATIVE ITEMS

Now that you have mastered the basics of jewellery making, try using the techniques to decorate other items. You can decorate almost any everyday item with beads to create unusual gifts and feature pieces.

ABSTRACT DECORATION

This hanging decoration was put together by suspending lengths of clear string threaded with beads and polished glass from a piece of driftwood. Wrapping the glass in fine wire adds an extra decorative touch.

GLASS AND WIRE

You can string beads on colourful wire, then wrap them around clear glass. Here, they are decorating a vase, but you could also put them on drinking glasses, perfume bottles or bath oils to make unique gifts. Vary the combinations of beads and gauges of wire for different effects.

BEADED CURTAIN

Thread beads onto clear string to make a bead curtain. Coloured glass or plastic beads will look really pretty hung against a window so that they sparkle in the sunlight.

PHONE CHARMS AND KEYRINGS

You can create small charms for your mobile phone by threading beads onto cord or leather ribbons. These are cheap and simple to make, so you can change them whenever you like! Use the techniques used to make the safety pin charm bracelet on page 30 to create a bead keyring.

GIFT-WRAP

Beads can also be used to jazz up gift wrapping. Pick beads in a colour to tone with the wrapping paper and fasten to a bow for a really classy look.

OTHER DECORATIVE ITEMS

GLOSSARY

abstract – Colours and shapes used to create an effect, rather than represent reality.

amulet – A charm, usually worn around the neck or carried in a pouch, believed by some people to ward off evil.

Art Deco movement – Art style, popular in the 1920s and 1930s, famous for its geometric shapes.

Art Nouveau – Art style, popular at the turn of the 20th century, famous for its intricate form and flowing curves.

cameo – A carving of a profile of someone against a different colour background

charm – A small decorative piece, often worn hanging from a bracelet.

enamel – Substance made from special powdered glass, heated at high temperatures to give a highly colourful finish to metal.

facet – Flat polished surface cut onto a bead or stone.

filigree – Delicate and intricate twisted wirework, often in gold or silver.

fire-polished bead – A method used to make beads smooth and shiny, also called Czech beads.

geometric – A design with a regular pattern and shape.

metal oxide – A substance formed from a combination of oxygen and metal.

ochre – One of the earliest forms of pigment, made from earth in colours from light yellow, to red and brown.

pigment – A substance used to colour or paint.

symbol – An object, mark or character used to represent something; for example, a crucifix is a symbol worn by Christians.

threading – Joining a series of beads by running a thread, cord or ribbon through them.

torque – A necklace, bracelet or armband made of twisted metal.

LISTINGS

Crafts Council
44a Pentonville Road
Islington
London
N1 9BY
Phone: +44 (0) 207 806 2500
Fax: +44 (0) 207 837 6891
www.craftscouncil.org.uk

The Association of Contemporary Jewellery
PO Box 37807
London
SE23 1XJ
020 8291 4201
www.acj.org.uk

The Beadworkers Guild
42–46 Lower Gravel Road
Bromley
Kent
BR2 8LJ
020 8462 2625
www.beadworkersguild.org.uk

GBUK (Glass Beadmakers UK)
29 Boundary Close
Upper Stratton
Swindon
Wiltshire
SN2 7TF
www.gbuk.org